I0473200

Business Networking Success:

The 5 Easy Steps to Building Your Business Network

Without EVER Going to Another

Business Networking Group!!

Liz Cassidy

Liz Cassidy
Third Sigma International
Level 7, 320 Adelaide St
Brisbane
QLD 4000
Australia.
www.leadershipmasteryinstitute.com

This publication is designed to provide general accurate and authoritative information in regard to the subject matter covered. It is sold the understanding that the publisher is not engaged in rendering legal, accounting, or other specific professional services. If legal advice or other expert assistance is required, the services of a competent professional person should be sought.

Get Liz Cassidy's personal help – see page 69 for details

Contents

Get Liz Cassidy's personal help – see page 69 for details

Dedication

I dedicate this book to one of the greatest networkers I have ever known.

I wish he was still alive to read it.

Thanks Dad

Introduction

Some time ago I was asked to deliver a networking talk for a small group of professional women. After I completed the talk, the ladies told me that the way I introduced the concept of networking was different to what they understood networking to be.

I have heard the feedback many times in my business career that my approach to a topic is "different". I didn't remark on or do anything with this feedback, so I thanked them and left the "Networking Talk" on my hard drive with many of the other talks I have given.

I was asked to give another Networking Talk as part of International Women's Day 2012. This time the audience was to be 70 business and professional women working for an international resources organization.

I revisited the original talk, updated it, added more information and delivered the talk. The response was overwhelming.

70 women networking in a room can make a lot of noise. This room was overflowing with delighted giggles, laughter and almost girlish joy. This from a group of professional women, who supposedly had networked before, had been to networking events and knew how to "Network".

At the end of the function a number of ladies approached and hugged me – I do like to be hugged at the end of a talk or seminar. It is a great expression of appreciation and I'm a very huggy person – but the feedback that they gave me again was that my way of networking was "different". Each of them, at various times in their lives, had given up on networking because "it didn't work" and I had to agree with them.

Networking old style doesn't work.

Networking my style is completely different because I network On Purpose.

This time I took notice of the feedback, the warmth and delight in the room that day convinced me that indeed my way is different and that my way works. Hence this book.

I have learnt the power and strength of working as a woman, as a professional and business woman, albeit mostly in a man's world. Everything I do is from a female perspective. I have had to adapt the male model to suit what works for me.

I stumbled into my way of networking after trying various other styles and trying to be someone that I wasn't. Eventually I decided that I was going to be me - warts and all - and if they didn't like me, then they wouldn't exchange business cards with me and there would be no follow up relationship.

Once I decided to start networking my way things changed. My way of approaching people changed, I was much more comfortable and authentic and no surprises then my business changed and grew.

As people recognized what I was doing, they recognized where I was coming from, a place of total authenticity. Just as importantly they recognized that I was coming from a place of service.

So this book is written for those of you who want to learn how to network differently and who are tired of the Old Style Networking that doesn't work.

As I write I am imagining that you are a female reader, but the information and approach contained in this book is equally valuable for men who decided to give up on networking because you found that traditional networking didn't work for you either.

I have also written this book for those of you who are in sales, are business owners, or are entrepreneurs who value a wide network and understand that opportunities abound from the most seemingly innocuous or casual acquaintances.

However, if you have a technical skill and want to network internally in your organization to gain career advancement then you will find that the techniques and approaches I have included are easily adapted to suit your needs as well.

There are a number of activities in this book that I strongly encourage you to do, I have included a number of writing spaces that I urge you to complete and a number of pages where I will encourage you to reflect.

As with any other activity based change book; you will get out of this book exactly what you put into it.

This book is not designed to sit on your shelf or remain passively on your eReader. It is designed to sit on your desk, beside you, to be written over, scribbled on and used. If you are downloading it as an e-book, then I encourage you to take a sheet of paper and where there is an activity to do, write on the sheet of paper and complete the activity for yourself.

Again, you will get out what you put in. If you do the activities and the exercises, you will make a huge change in

Get Liz Cassidy's personal help – see page 69 for details

the number and quality of your business relationships.

You will build new relationships. You'll increase the level of service that you offer to people and if you practice the techniques and approaches and get really good at what I teach you here then you will also increase your income because the more you network properly and effectively the more valuable you become.

Chapter 1

Business Networking Groups & Why I Avoid Them Like the Plague

Before we get into the concept of networking itself, let's look at how we relate to other people that we have just met.

The first thing we do is hold out our right hand (usually) we shake hands with them and say

"Hi I'm Liz".

In turn they generally hold out their hand, we shake hands palm to palm and often we judge the person by that handshake.

> Is it firm and solid?
>
> Are they a two handed... grip-your-hand-and-try-to-control-you ...kind of handshaker?
>
> Do they have a limp fish handshake - are they a bit cold and clammy?
>
> Do they have a Not-Much-Substance kind of handshake? Or as my children say, do they have a granny handshake where there is nothing to hold onto apart from the tips of their fingers?

With that initial handshake we tend to make a superficial

judgment of the people we meet, but the handshake itself is only a ritual. This ritual came from the middle ages when travelers meeting on the road, either on horseback or walking, would hold out their right hands to show that they didn't have a dagger. In showing they weren't holding a dagger they were saying "You are safe with me. I will not attack you"

The handshake we recognize today evolved from showing that we aren't carrying a dagger and is a staple introduction in any business environment. Although today we would also recognize that there are many new ways to be stabbed in the back without a physical dagger!

Having a good firm grip is part of the greeting ritual and it is part of how we judge people. We also make initial assessments based on what they look like, their grooming, how confident they look and what posture they adopt.

We assess if they walk upright or are timid and cowering and add this to the data we gain from their handshake. In the first few seconds of meeting people we subconsciously sum up what we think of that person according to our internal criteria and bias.

If we compare relating to others like peeling an onion then the outer layer, the dry brown skin, is just a ritual like the handshake. We don't really know anything about the person because we haven't shared anything of ourselves with them.

When we are effectively and authentically networking then we start to share a little bit more about who we are and we find out a little bit more about the other person, we begin to get to the tasty and juicy inner core of the onion.

Get Liz Cassidy's personal help – see page 69 for details

Traditional Networking

You may be familiar with the concept of business networking events.

Traditional networking events evolved as a process created by business men to meet other business men.

One of the things we know about human evolution is that the men went out as hunters, they were warriors. They would go out, target their prey, hunt down their prey, kill their prey and bring home their prey for their women folk to cook and feed the community.

In the meantime the women folk sat at home in the caves or around the camp, gathered nuts and fruit, looked after the children, looked after other people's children and basically provided a caring and nurturing service to their community group.

One reason (among many) that women may well take over the world of "virtual enterprises" is that they seem to have a greater instinct for networking. And the unfettered-by-machismo males who have taken to networking will do better than those who shun it as "sissy stuff." But truth is, it has always been the age of "networkers"; and in an era where organizations depend more and more on tenuously connected outsiders to get the job done, it will only become so.
Tom Peters

Let's now extrapolate that human evolution model to traditional networking. Whereas the men folk used to go out to hunt woolly mammoths or sabre tooth tigers, today they go out to business networking functions to hunt.

The menfolk went out because it was "business men" who had businesses and it was business men who went networking. They scoured the attendance list in advance and

Get Liz Cassidy's personal help – see page 69 for details

highlighted and pinpointed who their prey would be. Armed with a pocket full of business cards they hunted down their prey; shoved their business card at their prey and then went home to their women folk with a nights networking well done.

That's what my experience of traditional networking is.

When I started my business, I went to a number of these traditional networking events. I don't know if you have ever smelt desperation but desperation does have a unique smell, and it is repulsive. These networking events were full of other small business owners desperate to hunt down their prey, desperate to get a new client and to shove their business cards at these people. There was a lot of swopping of business cards around and monologue sales pitches and there was very little interest shown in who the other person was, or what their cares or struggles were.

I found these networking events disheartening. I found very little interest in me as a person, my needs or the problems that I needed to have resolved.

Often I would go home and have a shower because I felt dirty as if I had been covered in the slime of others' desperation.

I am not a quitter but eventually I said to myself, "I'm no good at networking, there is no point in me going to these networking events" and so I stopped going.

You may relate to my experiences with traditional networking. There is probably a very good reason why you have bought this particular book. Maybe you have decided to give networking one more try before you give up on it completely.

If that is the case, I applaud you.

There is a good chance you are reading this because you too have gone home to have a shower after another *fruitless networking event.*

That is what traditional networking is to me.

Let's look at what networking is not.

Networking - when done properly - is not a competition to hand out or collect business cards. Nor is it a sales pitch about you, your product and your business where all you do is wax lyrical about you and make sure that anyone within earshot knows all about you.

So now we know what it isn't.

Before I tell you what it is and how we network effectively, let's look at why we network in the first place.

Get Liz Cassidy's personal help – see page 69 for details

Chapter 2

Being on Purpose

So what is networking?

Networking is an opportunity and a process to develop long term relationships **On Purpose.**

On Purpose

What does "On Purpose" mean?

It may mean that if you run a business then your purpose is:

- ☝ To build your revenue, or
- ☝ To build your client base, or
- ☝ To build your reach and your influence, or
- ☝ To create a stable income for your family.

Any of those or something entirely different may be your purpose.

Let's say you are working in the community sector, then your purpose there may be community service, for example;

- ☝ Ending domestic violence,
- ☝ Ending child abuse,

- Fire fighting, or
- Surf lifesaving

In this case your purpose will be a community related purpose.

If you have a job or a profession, being "on purpose" may be:

- To extend your client base, or
- To increase your revenue streams in your business, or perhaps
- To get promoted.

Each of us has our own purpose and a reason to go out and meet other people and that purpose is unique to us.

I am going to ask you to take a few minutes and to make a note of what purpose you may have in building your network because if you do not have a purpose there really is no point in reading the rest of this book!

Without a purpose and without a reason the rest of this book is an academic exercise.

Take a few minutes now, reflect and note down below or on a separate sheet of paper, what your purpose for networking is.

My purpose in building my network of long term relationships is…

Get Liz Cassidy's personal help – see page 69 for details

Long Term Relationships

Let's also look at that phrase *long term relationships*. The element of traditional networking and networking events which struck me as being particularly repugnant was the short term and transactional nature of the interactions. The focus was on who is in the room right now and in answering the question 'who is useful to me *right now?"*

When we network effectively and are looking to the longer term, then we must acknowledge that the person in front of us right now may not be *useful to us* right now, but we acknowledge our higher purpose and that in looking to build long term relationships we are here instead to *serve them* and to be *useful to them.*

And this is the crux of Networking On Purpose; we turn the whole idea of traditional networking upside down and inside out.

- We seek to serve, rather than to hunt.
- We solve problems, rather than gain business card trophies.
- We aim to be of use, rather than to be a user.
- We connect, rather than transact.
- We are giving, rather than receiving.
- We are generous, rather than desperate.

Get Liz Cassidy's personal help – see page 69 for details

Get Liz Cassidy's personal help – see page 69 for details

Chapter 3

Who Is In My Network?

We all know many people. Sometimes we choose to forget those we know or dismiss them as being irrelevant. However, when we are networking with a focus on our higher purpose then there are very few people who we cannot serve over the longer term.

I am going to ask you in the next few pages to have a look at the headings of groups of people you may have met, and for each group, write down at least three contacts

You may not be able to write in three names under all those headings.

Perhaps you don't go to church, perhaps you didn't go to university, and perhaps you don't go to a gym. That's OK.

Where you have a blank category write down more names for one of the other headings.

Pretty soon you have between thirty and forty names written down without much effort.

I encourage you now to take time out and just start writing names and as before, On Purpose. What you will get out of this book is directly proportional to the effort you put into it.

Take a few minutes before you go further in this book, write

Get Liz Cassidy's personal help – see page 69 for details

down some names, test yourself and see how many you can write down.

At the networking event I described previously in the introduction, I talked about the 70 professional women and the volume in the room. One of those ladies wrote down 53 names in five minutes. She focused and started writing, so why don't you do that now?

You don't know the people who know the people you know
Liz Cassidy

Look at each of these groups below and write 3 names for each.

- ✓ School Friends
- ✓ School teachers
- ✓ University friends
- ✓ University Lecturers
- ✓ Work Colleagues – Present
- ✓ Suppliers – Past
- ✓ Work Colleagues – Past
- ✓ Supplier – Present
- ✓ Customers
- ✓ Parents of Children Friends
- ✓ Sporting Clubs
- ✓ Church
- ✓ Community Organizations
- ✓ Family
- ✓ Casual Acquaintances

Did you do it? Did you write some names? If you didn't, do not read any further, go back to the previous page and write down some real names of real people who you have met.

Now choose one of those people, someone you remember; perhaps someone from your childhood or someone you met at your own child's school; perhaps you will choose a current work colleague or someone you previously worked with.

Write down notes to describe the specific skills, abilities and attributes of the person you have chosen.

Write down what you think is great about that person, just for that one person.

Go on... do it...

As you look at your description of that person, I would ask you to consider...

Would you be happy to recommend that person or tell someone in your network about that person and how good they are at what they do?

Sure you would, because right now you are focused on their skills, attributes and abilities.

The important thing is, now that you have thought about that person and how good he is at what he

Your power is almost directly proportional to the thickness of your Rolodex, and the time you spend maintaining it. Put bluntly the most potent people I've known have been the best networkers -- they "know everybody from everywhere" and have just been out to lunch with most of them.
Tom Peters

does. Let's say you chose a Plumber who turned up on time, was neat and tidy, did a good job, cleaned up the job after himself and charged a reasonable price.

Now suppose one of your friends or a work colleague said to you. "I have a bathroom problem at home and I need a plumber". Wouldn't that plumber be front of mind and wouldn't you be comfortable in saying "Hey I can tell you about a great plumber "

What you just did was solve your friend's problem and you recommended someone you thought highly of. You were of service to your friend by solving her problem and you were also of service to the great plumber by giving him a new customer.

You cemented 2 relationships and created a new connection between your friend and the plumber. You were generous and unselfish to both. You networked effectively.

Interestingly, as women, and often as business people we

don't tell people what our own skills, attributes, or our abilities are. We assume they know or they should know.

However I have to tell you.
People don't know what you are great at.

Often people don't know how good you are because you hide your light under a bushel.

Isn't that a wonderful old fashioned phrase? A bushel is a biblical measure of weight. When you put a weight on your light no one will see it.

What we do when we start to *Network On Purpose* is to lift the bushel and allow our light to shine, without being arrogant or boastful, and how we do that is quite special and interesting.

Wouldn't it be wonderful if someone focused on you in the same way as in our previous example of the plumber?

Wouldn't it be great if other people recommended you as a solution to a problem?

Wouldn't it be great if every one of those people in your network thought of you that way and you were front of mind for whatever problems come up that you can solve?

That's what Networking On Purpose is.

The more people who know you and think highly of you, the more effective your network is, the more likely it is that they will tell their friends and colleagues about you.

My extended network is huge, but the number of people I know personally and who know me personally is relatively

Get Liz Cassidy's personal help – see page 69 for details

small. They in turn know a lot of people and they are happy to talk about me and what I do.

Why?

Because I have told them about what I do and I have provided services to them.

So let's re-examine who is in your network.

Because you don't know the people who know the people who know you; you don't know yet who has a problem that only you can solve. It is only by serving

Your network is all the people you know; and all the people who know you; and all the people who know them; who they can recommend you and your services to.

your existing network of connections, building new connections and educating them on what you do so well then they can reach out to their larger network on your behalf.

Get Liz Cassidy's personal help – see page 69 for details

Chapter 4

Where Do I Network?

The interesting thing about networking is that it is something that we do every day quite naturally. Every time we leave home, we are networking. Everywhere we are talking to or communicating with or relating to other people we are networking.

There is no time where we are not communicating with other people that we are not building our network.

We can network in the coffee shop with a colleague or a friend; we can do it in a pub. Some of my most effective networking has been done standing at the side of a cricket pitch as I cheered my son's cricket team. My son played for the "D" level cricket team. He is not on the "A" team so there is lots of opportunity to talk to other parents whilst the kids are running round chasing the ball and trying to do the fielding. There is *a lot* of down time when you are watching the "D" cricket team!

We can network when we attend training courses and conferences; we can do it in the park; we can network at airports or we can network over a water-cooler in the office kitchen; we can network on public transport or we can network in a doctor's waiting room.

Get Liz Cassidy's personal help – see page 69 for details

Anywhere there is another human being there is an opportunity to relate to someone else, to find out what their problems are and perhaps even to solve their problems.

There are endless opportunities to connect and be of service to others.

I tell a story of a time where I was changing the tire on my car; I had just picked up my 14 year old daughter from her surf lifesaving patrol at the beach. As I was leaving the surf club car park I heard a rumble, it wasn't a comforting sound. I stopped at the traffic lights, moved on a bit... the rumble continued... When I parked I found the rear tire was flat. I was on a busy main road and my teenage daughter encouraged me, as only a teenager daughter can, to move off into the side road where no-one could see us. As a woman with a flat tire the one thing I didn't want to do is move off onto a side road. I wanted to be where someone will see me and that person will stop and help me.

I can change a tire. It's been quite a few years since I've done it but I can still change a tire. *I just don't want to change a tire any more.*

I proceeded to open the car trunk and get the spare wheel out, loosened the nuts on the wheel and set about finding out where the jack went and as luck would have it a true gentleman walked up and said, "I noticed you as I was driving past, would you like some help?"

Oh joy, my prayers answered!

I found out after I shook the gentleman's hand that his name was Malcolm and he had been in Australia three years. He was from South Africa and at that point the conversation moved on to other things, as Malcolm was teaching my teenage daughter how to change a car tire. He was solving a problem he guessed she was going to have in the future. I appreciated him doing that but the point of the story is that you can network anywhere, even on the side of a busy main road with a flat tire.

There is nowhere you can't network because networking is a natural human interaction. You meet people, you shake their hands and you start the ritual of finding out who they are, what is important to them and what problems they have that you can solve.

You start to peel the relationship onion with each person that you meet.

So, that's where we network.

Everywhere!

Think of all the places you go every single day, write some of them down on a separate sheet of paper. Think of the places that you go to where you see people and there is an opportunity for you to turn around and say hello. Take a few minutes and write them down.

Get Liz Cassidy's personal help – see page 69 for details

Chapter 5

What Do I Bring When I am Networking?

What do you bring to *everywhere*?

The most important thing you can bring when you are networking is YOU!

The most critical and useful thing you can do is to show up.

Show up alert, interested and positive.

YOU! How do you show up?

I have an associate who dumps all her negativity and problems on me each time we meet. Her whining is endless. While my feelings towards her are (were) sympathetic, I do not see her as a Problem Solver. She is not front of mind when someone I meet has an issue even if her skill set is the right one to resolve the problem. In my mind her brand is one of Complainer - she is not a Solution.

Think of how you show up.

What is your brand?

How do people perceive you?

When we show up as flexible, positive and solutions focused; that is the memory we leave. We imprint that brand on the consciousness of our connections.

Get Liz Cassidy's personal help – see page 69 for details

Equally, it we show up as someone who doesn't deliver then that is the imprint we leave.

I have 2 clients who each experienced a disappointing and troubling start to their employment with 2 separate multi-national organizations. Both were senior professionals and in each instance through various miscommunications and corporate mix-ups each arrived excited to their new roles only to find that the role wasn't what they had been promised. Each had the same experience. Each was handed a lemon!

One client chose to be flexible and made lemonade from the lemons he found himself holding.

His attitude was one of "Here is what I'm good at, what do you need doing?" and he set about building relationships throughout the organization ensuring that he met the influencers and that they knew what his skills and abilities were.

The following year he had an international transfer, and two promotions.

The other client took the mix-up as a personal slight on his professionalism and filtered every subsequent communication from his manager through the lens of "managerial incompetence". He told his story far and wide, internally and externally to his organization.

His bitterness is still palpable. He sucked the lemon - and he isn't going anywhere fast.

Pen and Paper

It would be useful, but not critical, when you are out meeting people that you have a pocket or a bag that you can put their business cards into.

It would also be useful if you carried a pen and paper to write down the other persons contact details, if you want to continue a relationship with them.

Equally, if they have a business card you can collect it and write down where you met them and what their problems are that you are going to solve.

This reverse approach - of collecting cards and contact details - sometimes causes a little consternation with people who are used to traditional networking which involves pushing your business card into another person's hand.

One evening, my husband and I went to a charity event hosted by a local business man. We were bored rigid by an individual who waxed lyrical about himself and how great he was and then pushed his business card into the top pocket of my husband's suit.   You can guess where that business card went. That individual didn't ask either of us what we do, what problems we have, or how he could serve us. The business card was relegated to the circular filing cabinet. Exactly where it belonged.

The fact that you have a business card does not mean that everyone you meet wants to take it from you. It is more useful to ask them for their contact details.

So if you don't have business cards how can you network effectively?

In any relationship, someone usually takes the lead whilst the relationship is young. If you have met someone that you think you can provide a service to or if you have met

Get Liz Cassidy's personal help – see page 69 for details

someone who can solve your problems, wouldn't it be useful that you had their contact details so that you can follow up with them? You can make the phone call, you can send the e-mail, and you can write the note.

On the other hand when you give them your business card you are left like a teenage girl, hoping that the cute boy will ring her. It may never happen and she may sit home alone and lonely and feeling unloved.

When you have their contact details you are like the teenage boy who has 'control' of the relationship. You can choose to pick the phone up, you can follow up with them, and you can set up another meeting date. You are in charge of the relationship, and you are in control.

What we don't want when you are networking is for you to be shoving your business cards around willy-nilly without qualifying the interest level of the person you are talking to, like the self-centered individual at the charity event I mentioned previously.

You will be collecting business cards or contact details from people that you have a genuine interest in, or people that you have formed a connection with.

Again, if they do not have a business card you can write down their contact details.

I was at a Family Business lunch a few weeks ago where I forgot to bring my business cards. Also I didn't have a pen and I met a new contact who I know I could help. He wanted to expand his business and needed finance. I have recently met a number of people in the private equity area, so I knew I could connect him to them and get some conversations started. He didn't have a business card either. (Neither of us had planned well for this event!) We had a laugh about this and after a bit of brainstorming together I took a photograph of his lapel name badge with my smart phone. After the event was officially over I was talking to one of the event sponsors who works in the small business area of a national bank. He asked for my card, again I apologized that I was totally underprepared for this event, and told him the story of my new connection whose lapel badge photo I had taken. He was very interested in the man and wanted to make that connection himself. Because I had the photo in my phone I was able to help him to make the connection. He followed up with my new contact afterwards to talk about how the bank could help with expanding his business through a financing model.

So the morale of that story is:

It doesn't matter if you don't have all the tools of the networking trade with you, just show up and care!

Grooming

What do I mean by grooming?

You really do not want to be like the gentleman I sat beside on an airplane for thirteen hours, who had gross body odor. I did not want to connect with him. I truly didn't. So make sure your grooming is impeccable.

Do you need to be dressed in a power suit? Not at all. You dress appropriately for the activity you are doing, and for the memory you want to leave. For a kids sports match you wear comfortable clothing, and for an Executive lunch you can wear your power suit.

Business Cards

Finally and least importantly, you may bring along some business cards. If you do not have business cards – I went for almost eighteen months without business cards and I was probably at my most effective as a networker at that time - then it doesn't matter.

So what to bring when you are meeting people?

- You,
- An alert interested brain - with a positive attitude,
- A pocket for business cards,
- Pen and paper,
- A well groomed body.   And if you have them,
- Business cards

Get Liz Cassidy's personal help – see page 69 for details

Chapter 6

What's Involved in Networking?

You are going to be surprised to hear that what's involved in networking is communicating with genuine interest in other people and to get to know them and their needs better. Just think of the old saying:

"A stranger is just a friend I haven't met yet."

When we are caring about other people, we are networking and when we are Networking On Purpose we C.A.R.E.

C Create a sharing atmosphere,

A Ask open questions,

R Relate to their experience, and

E Enjoy yourself.

When we are Networking On Purpose we are relating with care.

After this it is simply technique.

Get Liz Cassidy's personal help – see page 69 for details

Emotional Bank Accounts

Imagine that you have a bank account which you deposit money into. A rainy day comes and you need to make a withdrawal. Because your bank account is in credit, then you have funds available to withdraw. If you have not made any previous deposits then you will have a much more difficult time making a withdrawal. You will be overdrawn and will owe the bank money. You will be in debt.

Now imagine that you have an emotional bank account. When someone does a good deed for you or provides an unexpected service they make a deposit into your emotional bank account. They have a credit in your account which allows them to make withdrawals. You have a warm regard for them, and perhaps later if they need you to help them you are happy to do so.

This is how human relationships work naturally, even though it sounds rather transactional when I describe it this way. However, we relate naturally to each other by making deposits and withdrawals in each of our relationships each day.

Dan Ariel describes this natural interaction of wanting to help each other from a scientific perspective in his book "Predictably Irrational"

If you have no credit in your emotional bank account in terms of your relationships and someone asks for help or a favor then they go into debt to you. You may feel that they owe you, or you may feel resentful toward them. However you will gladly give to those who have made prior deposits and have a credit in your emotional bank account.

When you are Networking On Purpose then you are making regular deposits into other people's emotional bank accounts; to the point where they will want to give back to you, with interest.

However; it is not easy make deposits or to solve other people's problems or to provide a service for them if they don't know what you are good at, and if you don't know what their problems and challenges are.

At this point I must make sure that I reiterate that you take a long term view of your relationships.

Most of us can smell manipulation mile away.

If you choose to be manipulative and make deposits for short term gain then you may well find that the Emotional Bank Account is closed for future withdrawals.

Networking for Introverts

When we relate to others and to their experience we take the focus of ourselves and on to them. Introverts may feel stressed at the thought of going to traditional networking meetings. Since I am advocating that you don't have to go to traditional networking meetings again you don't need to stress over this anymore. You may still *choose* to go to these meetings, but your approach will be very different.

You don't have to go to traditional networking functions again.

There is some erroneous thinking that introverts are socially inept.

Not at all. Introverts get their energy from social downtime and from being alone. Generally Introverts prefer for others break the ice, however professionals who are introverts learn to talk about business and professional issues with others who they don't know well.

Equally Introverts tend not to share much of their emotions, as these are private and personal. Introverts generally prefer to have close intimate long term relationships rather than many superficial relationships which are more the domain of extraverts. Using this Networking On Purpose approach *you will now be able to work within your natural personality preferences.*

You will be talking to others in a natural one-one relaxed and caring way. This is ideal for introverts who tend to consider before speaking and who prefer to communicate in small intimate groups or in quieter settings.

The Steps in Networking On Purpose

There are 5 core steps in networking effectively when we take the attitude that we are building long term relationships *on purpose*.

1. Break the Ice
2. Position yourself as the expert
3. Identify their problem
4. Solve their problem
5. Follow Up

Let's explore each of these in more detail.

Get Liz Cassidy's personal help – see page 69 for details

Step 1. Break the Ice

At this point we move into sharing and more intimacy with others. Up until now we have stayed at the "Hi, I'm Liz, how are you?" ritualistic level of relating to others. We are going to get a little bit deeper into the center of the 'relating to others onion', which means it's going to be a bit juicier and tastier.

When you meet someone for the first time it can be a challenge to find something to relate to. The weather is a staple subject and once that is exhausted where do you go next conversationally?

I used the CARE acronym earlier, now I am going to introduce another acronym to you to assist in breaking the conversational ice and to help you to find out common ground with new people. This simple tool is designed to help you to Relate to their experience more easily.

Used with skill, this tool will also help you to find out what motivates others and what their deep seated values are. When we talk to someone at a values level then we begin to have deeper and more meaningful conversations with them.

To break the ice conversationally we can use FORM.

This tool is not to be used as a tick sheet; it is rather more like a guiding light in our conversations. We can enter FORM at any letter and progress naturally and fluidly though with a view to getting to the M, early in the conversation.

What is FORM? And how do we use it?

F   Family

O   Occupation

R   Recreation

M   Motivation

When you meet someone for the first time, it is usual to notice apart from hand shake and posture, whether they are wearing a wedding band, approximate age and general other distinguishing features like ethnicity, accent etc.

This is what you do naturally.

When you are using FORM, you can ask questions about their Family. e.g. when I visit someone's office for the first time and I notice family snapshots or finger paintings on the wall, I am free to ask – what ages are the kids? Then I can chat about schooling and which subjects they like at school. If I meet someone with an interesting accent then I can ask if they recently came to this country and if they are here with their Family.

I strongly urge you NOT to use this as a young male engineer did at a night club after I ran a communication skills workshop. He sauntered up to an attractive girl and asked her if she wanted to start a Family with him, that night!! He got the response his question deserved.

Back on track, sometimes when I ask about children and what ages they are I find out that they are between 11-17 years old.

This naturally flows in to the R - Recreation.

I can easily and naturally chat about what sports their children are interested in and then I can truly empathize about driving around on weekends to various sporting events. I can also ask what my new contact does when she has time to spare for herself. So we start to peel the conversational onion and get to know a little about each other.

> *A friendship founded on business is better than a business founded on friendship.*
> **John D. Rockefeller**

The simplest part of FORM is the O-Occupation. Since we meet many people in a work environment, it is easy to talk to them about what their role is or how long they have been with the organization and where they were before etc. This is also a preferred point of entry into a conversation when on a training course, or conference. It is a point of common history.

From talking about work the conversation can flow back in to R-Recreation; what they enjoy doing out of work hours, which will often flow back into F-Family discussions.

With single people or non-parents this works equally as well but with less emphasis on F-Family and more on O-Occupation and R-Recreation.

What you really want to know is; what it is about their particular favorite Recreation, or about their Occupation, which attracted them so much. You want to get to the core of the conversational onion, and find out what M-Motivates them.

How you do this is to ask "What is it about (fill in the blank that has come up in conversation) that so appeals to you?"

Get Liz Cassidy's personal help – see page 69 for details

e.g. "What is it about tennis/golf/ running/ cycling/ rugby/ engineering/ architecture/ law/ base jumping / Montessori schools / Morris dancing / crochet / hill walking/Greco-Roman wrestling / learning Spanish…. etc. that so appeals to you?"

When you know this motivation then you know a lot about their values and what is important to them. Now you can relate to them at a much deeper values level.

Alternatively you may find that you don't relate to them at all at a values level. In which case you probably won't have a long term relationship with them and you have just saved yourself a huge amount of time.

Again this is what we naturally do in relationships, we get to know people over time and we get to know what makes them tick, maybe!

You simply accelerate the getting–to-know-you process using FORM.

As an extreme introvert who would rather chew my nails down to the knuckle than talk to a random stranger this conversational tool has been a life saver for me in business meetings and in social settings. It breaks the ice; I get to know more about the other person and what makes them tick; and I can relax while I do it.

They are also free to talk about their favorite subject – themselves.

Get Liz Cassidy's personal help – see page 69 for details

A caveat on using FORM is not to start at F and progress through the letters as if you were completing an application form. The conversation should flow from any starting point which feels natural and you can skip any of the letters if you find a point of common experience where you can dwell for a while.

Remember that you are *building a long term relationship on purpose;* you are not getting the groceries.

FORM is simply another tool you have in your interpersonal skills tool kit which you can choose to assist you to relate to another's experiences more easily.

People like people like themselves.

As you break the ice and begin to explore a little about your new contact you may find some points of common interest. As with any conversation you are now free to explore more and begin to develop a longer term relationship.

Step 2: Position yourself as the expert

Now we are going to get to the "pointy end" of networking. How do we actually do this?

From here on, for the rest of this book you may hear a little inner critic inside your head saying to yourself -

"Yes but..." or

"Yeah but Liz, I'm no good at networking", or

"Yeah but... I don't know what to say", or

It isn't just what you know, and it isn't just who you know. It's actually who you know, who knows you, and what you do for a living.
Bob Burg

"Yeah but...no body would be interested in me..."

"Yeah but, yeah but, yeah but...."

Let's just agree to no more "Buts" whilst you are reading and practicing the exercises here.

I have just had a cartoonist draw up a cheeky "No Buts!" logo for me which I have put on mugs and T-shirts so we can have "No Buts!" on our chests. That should get conversations and networking happening!

Remember back in Chapter 1 when you were thinking about someone on your list, and about how great that person is. You even wrote about their skills, their abilities and their attributes and I asked you "Would you like to have someone talking about you like that?"

You know a great way to be introduced is to have someone advocate for you like that.

The thing is; if we are telling friends and colleagues (and ourselves) how hopeless we are, and then they won't be able to tell other people how great we are, because they won't believe it.

What I am asking you to do is to shed your protective skin of "put yourself downishness". Instead you are going to tell people how great you are at what you do - without being arrogant or boastful.

What I am asking you to do is to talk, *honestly*, about what you do and the problems you solve. Effective networking is all about solving problems and building long term relationships.

So, how do you do it with "No Buts"? How do you introduce yourself?

- Find out what they do first.

- Tell them about you in the context of what they do and the problems they *might* have, (or that someone they know might have.)

For example if you are talking to a manager of a business (any level) then you can *guess* his problems *might* include:

1. Not enough time to get things done

2. Not getting staff to do exactly what he wants them to do

3. Not getting promoted fast enough

Or if you are talking to a small business owner then you can *guess* her problems might include:

1. Lack of direction – through sheer busy-ness

2. Not enough time to do everything she wants to get done

3. Lack of money / not enough customers

When you meet someone new and you find out what they do then you can describe the three problems that you solve in very generic terms.

As a natural part of a conversation they may ask "What do you do?"

The conversation ending trap is to name your job title, or to put yourself down, in the manner of "I'm an engineer" or worse "I'm just an engineer".

There are many types of engineer, bio-medical, mechanical, civil etc.

Instead of giving your title or function tell them the three general solutions that you provide that address their problems. These general solutions describe your skills, abilities and attributes - at a reasonably high level.

e.g. For the Business Owner we looked at previously I personally might say

"What I do is I sit down with Business Owners one-on-one and help them to work out where they want their business to go[1] , how to get the right quality of paying customers[3] , so that they can actually have some time off[2] and enjoy their family and their weekends. Now tell me about you, what do you do...?"

I know business owners don't take time off to enjoy their family and their weekends, and most small business owners want more good quality customers.

So you show how you can be of service to her *or to someone she knows* who has those problems.

You are not being boastful; you are simply expressing honestly what you do.

Your approach will keep the same pattern but will change

slightly according to who you are talking to.

If I am talking to a small business owner, I am not going to talk to her about leadership paths and leadership channels, because there may be only her and her immediate staff.

To summarize

You identify three of their generic problems by the three generic solutions you provide.

"Oh, what I do is….., and now tell me about you - what do you do?"

This way you are not boasting about yourself. You are presenting yourself as the potential solution for their problem or for the problems of someone in their network.

You don't know who they know and you don't know whose problem you may be able to solve.

We are not serving anyone at all if we don't tell them honestly what we can do to help them. In fact, we are being downright selfish and doing them a disservice. There is someone out there who has got a problem, who needs you and if you don't tell them that you can solve their problem, frankly you are being selfish.

I have put an example below which I have written from my perspective, as if I were talking to the manager in a business who I described before.

e.g. "You know how as a manager you might across some people who just won't listen to you [2]? Then there might be times when you get to Friday when you've still got your weekly list left to do [1], or you might just want to get that promotion [3].

Well what I do, is I work confidentially, with professionals and managers like you to help them grow their people and influencing skills. [Solved problem 2] Be more effective with their time. [Solved problem12]) and to get where they want to go faster. *(Solved Problem 3)*

And I've got a bit of a reputation for cutting through. Now that's enough about me, tell me a bit more about what you do"

I have also told them through the last sentence "don't even bother talking to me if you want someone to be nice and fliff flaff with you". If they want to continue the conversation with me then they are telling me they want to get to know me better.

Now it's your turn...

Pick an imaginary someone that you might meet in your working life. Write down three problems that you would imagine this person would have, just as I have done previously with the small business owner and the manager previously here in this chapter.

Problem 1..

Problem 2..

Problem 3..

For each of the generic problems above write down your solutions describing your skills, abilities and attributes

Solution 1..

Solution 2..

Solution 3..

and I ....

(something for them to remember you by)

Get Liz Cassidy's personal help – see page 69 for details

Let's put the two parts together seamlessly into your initial introduction script.

"You know how you

....

....

....

Well, what I do is

....

....

....

and

I...

You will become more adept at saying

"You know how ... .?   Well what I do is..."

As you meet different people with different generic problems you can practice slightly different variations on the theme until you settle on your unique set of skills, abilities and attributes that you are happy for your network to tell their friends and associates about.

I am sure you will come up with some outstanding solutions once you stop "Yeah But-ting" on yourself.

Now you are starting to get an idea of how to tell people what problems you solve, and when they come across someone with that problem, they can say "Oh! I know who you should call..." on your behalf.

Educate them first in what you do, and then they will remember you.

That's what you are starting to learn how to do.

Now I am going to teach you how to ask them what their specific problem might be.

Get Liz Cassidy's personal help – see page 69 for details

Step 3. Find their Specific Problem

This introduces YOU as the Centre of Influence.

In your conversations with new people after you have broken the ice with CARE and have gotten to know them a little bit using FORM. Now, you can begin asking them

"What is your biggest problem or challenge at the moment?"

That's all you have to do.

Can you personally solve their problem? If the answer is Yes you can, then make an offer to help.

Position yourself as a center of influence - the one who knows the movers and shakers. People will respond to that, and you'll soon become what you project.
Bob Burg

Sometimes you will come across people where that question is either not appropriate or they can't see past their busy-ness to what their problems are. In this case it may be useful to offer to solve a problem that you think they might have.

Small Business Owners and Entrepreneurs

I mentioned previously that most small business owners are looking for more good quality paying customers.

If you don't feel comfortable yet asking "What is your biggest problem or challenge at the moment?" or if they are so overwhelmed with the problems of their business that they can't answer then an alternative may be to focus on the one problem that you guess they might have.

Get Liz Cassidy's personal help – see page 69 for details

e.g. "What does your ideal customer look like?"

This is a much easier question for business owners and entrepreneurs to answer.

It also gives you a mental picture of who they are looking for and a checklist of how to ease a perennial problem.

Large Business Owners or Senior Executives

A similar question with a slightly different slant is

"What kinds of business opportunities are you looking for, right now?"

This question can apply to a senior executive or to the owner of a business. These people may be more focused on buy outs, take overs, joint ventures, or expanding supply arrangements and may be more focused on growth opportunities rather than overcoming specific challenges.

e.g. one of my clients managed a large parcel of land on behalf of the company he works for.
Another client runs a beef cattle business.

It never occurred to me to introduce them until one day the Land Manager mentioned that he wanted to increase the yield of the land he manages. The conversation developed and he mentioned beef cattle.

I talked separately to my Beef Cattle client who is incredibly busy and has never mentioned land availability to me before as an issue. I asked him if he needed access to more land. I got permission from both to share their contact details and introduced them.

Note that I did not provide a paid service to either in this instance. I did serve both generously and unselfishly. I made

Get Liz Cassidy's personal help – see page 69 for details

a deposit in each of their emotional bank accounts.

The result? Yes, I have had good quality business lead referred to me from one of them.

The reason you ask about their specific issues or problems, is that when you know what they need then you can be the source of their solutions. You can become a Center of Influence for their business.

When you are front of mind, the next time they need what it is that you provide then you will get the call. If you are not font of mind, then someone else will get the call.

Get Liz Cassidy's personal help – see page 69 for details

Step 4. Solve their problem

When you make an offer to help you are either personally, or through your business expertise solving their problem. This is a commercial agreement.

But if you are not their solution, that's OK too. You don't have to be Super Man or Wonder Woman and wear red underwear on the outside of your hose.

If you know someone who can solve their problem, offer to make the introduction, just like we did with the plumber example earlier.

And if you can't think of anybody, be honest, say "look I can't think of anybody who can help right now but if there is anybody in my network, would you like me to introduce you?"

Let's imagine you meet a lady today whose biggest problem is not being able to save money but you may not be good with budgets and financial planning. Do you think you could find somebody in the next two days who is any good at budgeting? Of course you can. Why? Because you have found someone with a need, you don't have a solution so it might be to both your benefits to find that person and you made a commitment that you are going to.

If in the next couple of days you haven't found someone, then just get back to her so that you are not going to leave her wondering what happened or where you went to. You close the loop with her. Even if you are not able to solve her problem you can still make a deposit in her Emotional Bank Account by getting back to her.

Once you do provide a solution or an introduction to

Get Liz Cassidy's personal help – see page 69 for details

someone who can provide the solution, you will have made another deposit in her emotional bank account. Do you think she will *remember* you? Yes of course. And the human Law of Reciprocity is that she will want to do something for you in return.

As a professional and a business woman the ideal would be for her to refer a client to you, someone else whose problem you can solve (for a fee!)

If you have not told her clearly what it is that you do, what your skills abilities and attributes are, she will not be able to serve you in turn. You need to make sure, as you will do in future, that you let people know what you do through your introductory script

"You know how ......?   Well what I do is..."

Your challenge now and for the rest of your career; is to conversationally ask each new person you meet

- "What's your biggest business problem or challenge at the moment?"
- Listen to what they say...
  If you can fix their challenge, offer to!
- If you cannot fix their challenge by yourself then offer to find someone who can.
- Close the loop with them inside 2 days.

When we introduce 2 people the responsibility of their on-going relationship rests with them. We have done our bit in generously serving both.

However if they are not a good fit in terms of solutions they can work that out for themselves.

Our role is complete once the introductions are made.

Step 5. Follow Up

Why do we follow up? We follow up to extend and deepen the relationship and perhaps to move closer to solving their problem.

In traditional networking terms a follow up was essentially a sales call.

The currency of real networking is not greed but generosity.
Keith Ferrazzi

In Networking On Purpose a follow up is purely to find out more about their problem and to find if you have common ground and if there is anything more for you to talk about.

Remember that Networking On Purpose is about building long term relationships *On Purpose*. It is not about short term transactions. We are not selling a used car. We are developing a relationship and hopefully moving from first date through to marriage.

You have met a new person, you have **C**reated a sharing atmosphere, you have **A**sked open questions, you have **R**elated to their experience and you have had some fun and **E**njoyed yourself.

You have related to them with C.A.R.E.

And as you leave you have gotten their contact details e.g.

"By the way do you have a business card with you?"

Remember that you don't have to take the contact details of every person you meet, if there is no connection or you don't want to pursue the relationship.

You may or may not have given them your business details

Get Liz Cassidy's personal help – see page 69 for details

or business card. You may or may not have set a follow up appointment there and then. If there is an instant click and you identify a problem that you can solve - then get your calendar out and set a next meeting straight away.

Imagine that you just met someone new and you have returned to your office with their contact details. You may be wondering what to do next.

The first thing you do is record their details into some kind of database.

Microsoft Outlook provides a contacts database or there are a number of CRM packages which if you have a business I would suggest you invest in a good one. Even a simple spread sheet would be fine to record contacts.

You can record their contact details; including where and when you met the person, what their specific problem is and what you have done to follow up with them.

Obviously at this point you haven't done any follow up so let's look at that.

Follow Up Cards

In following up you want to imprint a warm memory of you in their minds.

A simple and most effective way to do this is to send an old fashioned hand written note to them shortly after you meet. [You could send an email, but frankly everyone does this, and there is nothing memorable about it.]

If you want to make a deposit into someone's emotional bank account then do something that no one else does - make them feel special.

My strong suggestion is that you create, or buy; some follow up cards; write a hand written note in blue ink; put it into a colored envelope and post it to them.

Because I do this so often, I have created a set of Follow Up Cards. There is a link at the back of this book if you want to get those cards and adapt them to suit your business. I have chosen some meaningful quotes and because I have made a connection with another person, I believe these quotes may also touch them.

I write a note, in blue ink, inside the card telling them what a pleasure it was to meet them, reminding them of who I am and offering to be of assistance to them in the future. At this point I also attach a business card if I have one.

It has happened in the past that I have received a phone call from someone in tears when they have opened my card. They have been having an awful day and my card has given them a lift. The tears were tears of gratitude.

When you start sending Follow Up Cards to your new contacts then within a few days of meeting you they will get a colored envelope in the mail with a handwritten note inside.

Do you think someone receiving a handwritten card with a very special quote on the front will remember you and think of you warmly? Of course they will.

People who put effort (and money) into a relationship are saying:

"Hey, you are worth something to me".

So I strongly encourage that you handwrite a card and post it to them.

Having some follow up cards already available in your car

or in a notebook holder is incredibly useful. That way you don't have to remember to go buy them after you have met a new person. You can also write the note to them with the relationship still warm in your mind.

Phone Call

The second follow up option is a phone call.

A phone call as a follow up usually has an intention behind it. You are phoning them to say,

"Let's meet again, let's take this relationship to a different level, let's find out more about each other and perhaps... let's do business"

You are making the phone call to set up another meeting, so the phone call is a further investment that I encourage if there is someone whose problem you can solve.

For those of you who are in business or in sales, remember, this is *not* a sales call.

It is a follow up phone call to explore if there really is a way that you can solve this person's problem. That shift in attitude and perspective might help you make the phone call a little more easily.

It is not a cold call and it is not a sales call. It is a phone call to set up a meeting to explore the relationship and to find out if there is something that you can do with each other in terms of extending your business relationship.

Email

The third follow up option is e-mail.

As with any e-mail this is a one way communication. It has no tonality. There is not really much investment in it and it is kind of a wishy-washy half-hearted follow up. It really has no content or substance. Email follow up is a bit like a blancmange layer on dessert. It's just a bland filling.

If you only sent them an e-mail – then you are not putting very much effort or investment into the relationship. So by implication you are sending the message that,

"Yes, I am following up with you, but all you are worth really is an e-mail."

It is nice to receive a follow up email but it's like having someone write Happy Birthday on the wall of your Facebook page. You don't value it anywhere nearly as much a handwritten birthday card or a cupcake with a candle in it.

Get Liz Cassidy's personal help – see page 69 for details

Meeting

The final follow up is a one to one meeting. If you can set up the meeting at the initial introduction it is far more useful and your follow up meeting is going to start warm.

However you can also set up the meeting during a follow up phone call. It will still be very effective.

It's all about people. It's about networking and being nice to people and not burning any bridges.
Mike Davidson

Remember too when you are following up; always follow up with courtesy and follow up with C.A.R.E.

You are **C**reating an atmosphere, you are **A**sking open questions you are **R**elating to their experience and you are planning on having fun and **E**njoying yourself.

This is the beginning of a long term relationship On Purpose.

Get Liz Cassidy's personal help – see page 69 for details

Chapter 7

Other Forms of Networking

Today many people are doing their networking online and that is great. You can build a relationship online through social media.

However psychologists are showing that the distance created by a keyboard and screen can affect the way we present ourselves to the online community.

As a result it is useful to be aware that the sooner you can take the relationship offline the sooner you can do business with the 'real' person.

By all means, start the relationship online. Start communicating with the person, finding out more about their needs and problems but then move the communication offline to the point of phone calls and meetings.

The sooner you can do that, the sooner you can be more effective in your networking.

Remember that Networking On Purpose is about finding out what other people's problems are and solving those problems for them either by you providing the service or by you introducing them to someone else who can solve that problem.

That can be done online, but it is much more effective for a *long term* relationship if you can do it offline. We want to move the relationship to a long term footing.

I hope that is useful and puts some context in around the online/offline aspect of networking.

Chapter 8

and Finally...

When you look at how many people you know today and how many of these relationships you have not nurtured, you may decide to make a few phone calls to these people first before you start to meet anyone new.

We all change, our circumstances change and our needs change.

Thus it is safe to assume that people you met a few years ago have moved on with their lives and businesses and have new problems for you to solve.

As with any other long term relationship, your business relationships need some time investment.

When you make a new contact make a diary note to keep in touch with them each 90-120 days by note, email, phone or via a meeting. A reasonable CRM program will help with this.

When you are serious about building your business network I suggest that you put aside a few hours each week, just for keeping in touch with people and for building relationships.

This may seem a lot of time in an already busy schedule. However, you know already that quality relationships are

Get Liz Cassidy's personal help – see page 69 for details

what make a business professional successful and the more time you invest in building relationships, the more successful you will become.

Simple and fast ways to keep in touch are to send newspaper clipping or extracts from business magazines, which may be pertinent. Perhaps you received information about an upcoming webinar from someone you trust that would be useful to members of your network, then you can pass this on. If you receive information about an upcoming conference, course, or lunch with an interesting speaker then this too can be passed on.

Being a center of influence does not need to take up a lot of time - when you are a little creative and think from a service perspective.

Obviously if you meet a new potential client or customer for your contacts then you can make an introduction.

It is time for you to start investing your time into your business and in your future success.

I urge you to shift the way you relate to your existing and new contacts. Use C.A.R.E. and follow the 5 steps to become a center of influence and a Problem Solver.

Become known as the person who solves their problems and they will reward you with their business referrals.

Good luck!

Get Liz Cassidy's Personal Help

Are you serious about building your business and/or your career?

There are so many things to think of in building your business that no one can know it all starting out.   From creating a strategy, implementing your strategy, do you need a board, recruiting your team, delegating, performance managing, keeping track of finances,…. Oh yes, then you have customers to take care of too!

And so it goes on.   Before you know it- you haven't seen your family in days.

All you wanted to do was have a profitable business but there is so much more to know and to DO!

Liz Cassidy is passionate about making life easier and simpler for Owners, Leaders and Managers and is making her **FREE 4 part "Build Your Business Faster" Training Program** available to you.

Use her free 4 part Video Training Program to accelerate your business, get more done and reduce your stress levels doing it.

Go to <u>www.LeadershipMasteryClub.org/</u> *TODAY*

Follow Up Cards -

These specially designed Follow Up Cards each have a quotation on the front and space for you to write your message on the inside. They will be treasured for months and years.

http://www.cafepress.com/lizcassidy/8623835

Get Liz Cassidy's personal help – see page 69 for details

About The Author

Liz Cassidy, Amazon #1 Best Selling author, is the founder of Third Sigma International and the Leadership Mastery Institute.

With 27 years industry and business experience in multinational, nationals and small business, in the UK and here in Australia within Production, Operations, Distribution Management, Sales and Professional Services in traditional and online businesses, there are not many aspects of Building, Leading and Managing a Business that Liz has not experienced and coached her clients in.

Now Brisbane based she travels to the USA extensively with her business and is recognized and acknowledged for her skill and ability in assisting her Executive Coaching clients to overcome business and leadership blocks.

Liz has been a guest on multiple local and national radio shows and has articles in a number of business magazines.

To talk Liz about speaking to your group or to coach you personally contact her via her website
http://leadershipmasteryinstitute.com

Get Liz Cassidy's personal help – see page 69 for details

Get Liz Cassidy's personal help – see page 69 for details

Other Books by Liz Cassidy

Job Interview Questions & Answers:
Your Guide to Winning in Job Interviews

Liz Cassidy brings another down to earth and matter of fact book to us. This time on Job Interview Question and Answers. This book is unashamedly a primer for Professionals on preparing for your Job Interviews.

It is succinct and cuts through to get to what the person on the other side of the desk needs to know about you to make that "YES" decision and to take a leap of faith on you.

This book is short on fluff and filled to the brim with tips, advice and How To's. Drawn from her experience training managers in interview skills and in coaching retrenched professionals through Career Transition, Liz Cassidy has a unique view of both sides of the Job Interview fence.

She is equally as unforgiving with interviewers "smart curve ball" questions as she is with sloppily prepared candidates. This book demands professionalism from both parties in the interview but is primarily a guide to professional candidates on how to deal with the real world of untrained, unaware and underprepared recruiters and interviewers.

Packed with real questions and with a focus on behavioral interviews Liz Cassidy's latest book will having you going into an interview prepared; and coming out of an interview glad that you read it!

You can Buy it on Amazon.com

Get Liz Cassidy's personal help – see page 69 for details

www.ingramcontent.com/pod-product-compliance
Lightning Source LLC
Chambersburg PA
CBHW071622170526
45166CB00003B/1154